TEXAS TEST PREP

Reading Workbook

STAAR Reading

Grade 2

ISBN 978-1478228165

CONTENTS

INTRODUCTION
For Parents, Teachers, and Tutors

About the Book

This workbook is designed to develop the skills that grade 2 students are expected to have. These skills are described in the Texas Essential Knowledge and Skills, or TEKS. The focus of the book is on developing reading comprehension skills, but the complementary writing and language skills are also covered.

Ongoing Reading Comprehension Practice

This workbook allows students to have ongoing practice as part of their homework routine. Without the stress of long complex passages and long question sets, students can develop the reading skills needed while gaining confidence and becoming familiar with answering reading comprehension questions.

Developing Core Skills

The state standards for Texas are known as the Texas Essential Knowledge and Skills, or TEKS. These standards describe what students are expected to know. Student learning is based on these standards throughout the year, and the state test includes questions that assess whether students have the skills described in the standards.

The skills described in the TEKS cover reading, writing, and language. Each passage in this workbook includes a Core Skills Practice exercise. Each exercise focuses on one key reading, writing, or language skill. By completing these exercises, students will develop the core skills that grade 2 students are expected to have.

Preparing for the STAAR Reading Test

In grade 3, students will take the STAAR Reading test. This workbook contains passages and question sets similar to those on the STAAR Reading test, but much shorter. These will prepare students for the types of questions they will answer on the state test. The Core Skills Practice exercises included with each passage will develop the core skills that students will need to perform well on the state test. The last passage in each set also has an extended-response question. This question will give students practice providing written answers and will ensure that students can understand, analyze, and respond to passages.

Reading Comprehension

STAAR Reading

Set 1

Instructions

Read each passage. Complete the exercise under each passage.

Then complete the questions on the next page. For each multiple-choice question, read the question carefully. Then select the best answer. Fill in the circle for the correct answer.

A Close Match

Adam and Juan took their places on the court. The ball began to fly and bounce off their rackets. The crowd turned their heads back and forth. Adam's friend Beth cheered each time he scored a point. Juan's coach Demi cheered each time Juan won a point. Juan finally won the game.

After the game was done, Juan walked to the middle of the net. Adam was quite upset about the loss. He really wanted to storm off the court. But he knew that it wasn't the right thing to do. He met Juan at the net.

"Good game," he said, as he shook Juan's hand.

"You too," Juan said. "You made it a tough match to win."

Adam still felt a little upset. But he was proud of himself for doing the right thing.

CORE SKILLS PRACTICE

You can tell a lot about characters by what they do. Think about what Adam does in the story. Do you think Adam is a good sport? Explain how you can tell.

_____

_____

_____

_____

_____

_____

1   Read this sentence from the passage.

He really wanted to storm off the court.

What does the phrase "storm off" suggest about Adam?

Ⓐ   He is tired.

Ⓑ   He is excited.

Ⓒ   He is angry.

Ⓓ   He is hot.

2   Who is the main character in the passage?

Ⓐ   Adam

Ⓑ   Juan

Ⓒ   Beth

Ⓓ   Demi

3   The main theme of the passage is about –

Ⓐ   always winning

Ⓑ   being a good sport

Ⓒ   practicing often

Ⓓ   trying your best

Polar Bears

Polar bears are large white bears that live in the Arctic. Their main diet consists of seals or large animals that wash up onto the shore. Because of the fat they eat from these creatures, there is rarely a need for the polar bear to drink water. This means that polar bears can survive on food alone. A polar bear eats an average of two kilograms of food per day. That's like eating 20 to 30 hamburgers a day!

CORE SKILLS PRACTICE

The author gives information on what polar bears eat and how much polar bears eat. Imagine you want to write a new report about polar bears. What else would you want to include in the report? Write a list of questions you could research and answer in your report.

1. _____

2. _____

3. _____

4. _____

5. _____

6. _____

1 Read this sentence from the passage.

That's like eating 20 to 30 hamburgers a day!

Why does the author most likely include this sentence?

Ⓐ   To suggest that polar bears eat hamburgers

Ⓑ   To show that hamburgers contain a lot of fat

Ⓒ   To show how much polar bears eat each day

Ⓓ   To suggest that polar bears should eat less

2 What is the passage mostly about?

Ⓐ   What polar bears eat

Ⓑ   What polar bears look like

Ⓒ   Where polar bears live

Ⓓ   Why polar bears are special

3 Which statement best explains why polar bears are able to survive without drinking water?

Ⓐ   They are large enough not to need water.

Ⓑ   They live in a very cold environment.

Ⓒ   They eat a large amount of fat.

Ⓓ   They eat food that washes up out of the water.

Busy Bees

There are twenty thousand known species of bees in the world. Different types of honey bees make up only seven of those species. The honey bee is believed to have come from Asia. However, scientists believe that some species could have come from Europe. Today, honey bees are used by beekeepers to help pollinate crops of flowers. They are also used to make honey and to make beeswax.

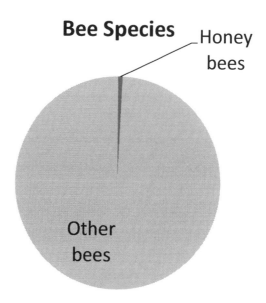

Bee Species

CORE SKILLS PRACTICE

The passage uses nouns and proper nouns. Nouns are general names for people, places, things, or ideas. Proper nouns name a certain person, place, thing, or idea. Complete the table by listing four nouns and two proper nouns from the passage.

Nouns	Nouns	Proper Nouns

1   Complete the web below using information from the passage.

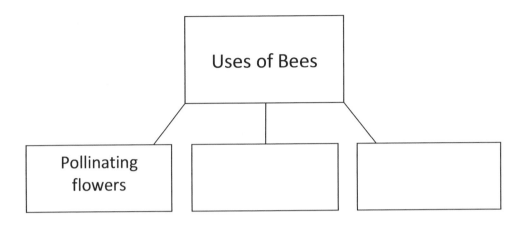

2   What is the main purpose of the graph?

Ⓐ   To show that only a few of all bee species are honey bees

Ⓑ   To show that honey bees have several uses

Ⓒ   To show that honey bees are decreasing in number

Ⓓ   To show that most honey bees come from South East Asia

3   The author probably wrote the passage to –

Ⓐ   warn readers about bees

Ⓑ   inform readers about bees

Ⓒ   persuade readers to keep bees

Ⓓ   teach readers how to find honey bees

Scrambled Eggs

Let's make some yummy scrambled eggs! There are six steps to making the perfect scrambled eggs. It's easy to do and they're always delicious. Let's do it:

1. Crack two eggs into a saucepan.
2. Add 1 teaspoon of butter and a splash of milk.
3. Turn on the hotplate. You should ask an adult to turn on the hotplate for you.
4. Use a wooden spoon to scramble the eggs and burst the yolks.
5. Keep mixing as the eggs cook. The eggs will be ready when they are no longer runny. They will have a light and fluffy finish.
6. Add some salt and a little bit of pepper. Your eggs are ready to be enjoyed!

CORE SKILLS PRACTICE

Read the first paragraph. The writer includes this paragraph to make the reader want to make scrambled eggs. Explain how the writer makes the reader want to make scrambled eggs.

_____

_____

_____

_____

_____

_____

1   Read this sentence from the passage.

Add 1 teaspoon of butter and a splash of milk.

What does the word <u>splash</u> show?

Ⓐ   A lot of milk should be added.

Ⓑ   The milk should be added quickly.

Ⓒ   Only a little bit of milk is needed.

Ⓓ   The milk must be added slowly.

2   What is the most likely reason the author says to ask an adult to turn on the hotplate for you?

Ⓐ   So the hotplate is on high enough

Ⓑ   So you do not harm yourself

Ⓒ   So the adult can help you mix

Ⓓ   So the adult can check if you did everything right

3   Which of the following is needed last?

Ⓐ   Eggs

Ⓑ   Pepper

Ⓒ   Milk

Ⓓ   Butter

Crash Landing

Dear Annie,

Today I fell off my bike. I was going too fast along a rough track. At first, I began to cry. I was worried my bike would be broken. Dad looked at it and said it was okay, and that I should be more careful. He made me sit down for a little while to make sure I was alright. But I knew I was fine because falling off didn't even hurt! After a little while, I wanted to go and ride my bike again. It's times like these that I'm glad Dad makes me put on a helmet and knee guards!

Later,

Stacey

CORE SKILLS PRACTICE

In this passage, the writer describes an event from her day. Write a paragraph describing an event from your day.

_____

_____

_____

_____

_____

_____

---

1   Read this sentence from the passage.

I was going too fast along a rough track.

What does the word <u>rough</u> mean in the sentence?

Ⓐ   Difficult

Ⓑ   Bumpy

Ⓒ   Old

Ⓓ   Smooth

2   Why does Stacey start to cry when she falls off her bike?

Ⓐ   She has hurt herself.

Ⓑ   She is scared that her father will be mad at her.

Ⓒ   She thinks that she has broken her bike.

Ⓓ   She doesn't know how she will get home.

3   What type of passage is "Crash Landing"?

Ⓐ   Short story

Ⓑ   Science fiction story

Ⓒ   Letter

Ⓓ   Fable

4   Why does Stacey say she is glad that her father makes her wear a helmet and knee guards? Use information from the passage to support your answer.

DIRECTIONS Be sure to:

- Write your answer in your own words.
- Write clearly.
- Check your answer after writing it.

_____

_____

_____

_____

_____

_____

_____

_____

Reading Comprehension

STAAR Reading

Set 2

Instructions

Read each passage. Complete the exercise under each passage.

Then complete the questions on the next page. For each multiple-choice question, read the question carefully. Then select the best answer. Fill in the circle for the correct answer.

Paper Planes

Ben sat at the table with Terry, neatly folding pieces of paper. They were making paper planes. Every plane Ben made was perfect. Terry, on the other hand, never seemed to make one that could fly. Terry tried to fly his latest plane across the room. It fell to the ground like it was made of lead. Terry banged his hand on the table.

"I'm not making any more planes!" Terry said.

Ben took Terry's plane and adjusted a few folds. It glided through the air!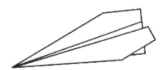

"Maybe I'll try just a few more," Terry said.

CORE SKILLS PRACTICE

Many stories involve cause and effect. The cause is the reason for an event. The effect is what happens. Answer the questions about cause and effect.

Why does Terry say he is not going to make any more planes?

_____

_____

What happens when Ben adjusts Terry's plane?

_____

_____

---

1   Which sentence from the passage contains a simile?

    Ⓐ   *They were making paper planes.*

    Ⓑ   *Every plane Ben made was perfect.*

    Ⓒ   *It fell to the ground like it was made of lead.*

    Ⓓ   *Terry banged his hand on the table.*

2   How does Terry most likely feel in the first paragraph?

    Ⓐ   Bored

    Ⓑ   Annoyed

    Ⓒ   Hopeful

    Ⓓ   Proud

3   Read this sentence from the passage.

    It glided through the air!

The word <u>glided</u> suggests that the plane flew –

    Ⓐ   smoothly

    Ⓑ   quickly

    Ⓒ   slowly

    Ⓓ   clumsily

My School Friends

 It's very important to have friends. They help you when you feel lonely. They are fun to share secrets with too. My best friends are Link, Beth, and Sally. They all go to my school and are in the same class as I am. Sally is my best friend as well as my cousin.

We always make sure to behave in class so the teacher allows us to sit beside each other. Sometimes we can't help but laugh with each other. Especially when Beth tells us jokes. She is the funniest friend I have. That is when the teacher makes us move apart.

CORE SKILLS PRACTICE

The narrator of the passage gives her opinion about friends. She says that it is very important to have friends. Do you agree that it is very important to have friends? Explain why or why not.

_____

_____

_____

_____

_____

_____

1   Which of the following is NOT a friend of the narrator?

    Ⓐ   Link

    Ⓑ   Anna

    Ⓒ   Beth

    Ⓓ   Sally

2   Why do the narrator and her friends behave in class?

    Ⓐ   So they get given good grades

    Ⓑ   So they can sit together

    Ⓒ   So they are allowed to talk

    Ⓓ   So they are not asked to stay after class

3   How is Beth different from Link and Sally?

    Ⓐ   Beth is the narrator's cousin.

    Ⓑ   Beth is in a different class.

    Ⓒ   Beth is a funnier person.

    Ⓓ   Beth is not as good a friend.

Dolphins

Dolphins are marine mammals. Many people mistake dolphins as being a type of fish. They look similar to fish and have fins, but dolphins are actually mammals. They do not have gills, while all fish have gills.

Dolphins are close relatives to both whales and porpoises. There are over 40 different species of dolphins. They are located worldwide, but live mostly in shallow and tropical waters. They are very intelligent mammals. They can be trained and are well known for being able to perform tricks. Dolphins are also carnivores. They eat fish and squid.

CORE SKILLS PRACTICE

This passage gives facts about dolphins. Facts are statements that can be proven to be true. Complete the list of facts by adding four more facts to the list.

Facts about Dolphins

1. They are mammals.

2. _____

3. _____

4. _____

5. _____

---

1   What is the main purpose of the first paragraph?

     Ⓐ   To describe what dolphins look like

     Ⓑ   To compare dolphins and fish

     Ⓒ   To describe where dolphins live

     Ⓓ   To show that dolphins are like whales

2   How are dolphins different from fish?

     Ⓐ   They live in the water.

     Ⓑ   They lack gills.

     Ⓒ   They have fins.

     Ⓓ   They eat meat.

3   Which detail from the passage best shows that dolphins are intelligent?

     Ⓐ   They can perform tricks.

     Ⓑ   They eat fish and squid.

     Ⓒ   They are located worldwide.

     Ⓓ   They mostly live in shallow water.

Davy Crockett

Davy Crockett was born on August 17th, 1786. He was born in Tennessee. He was known for being a brave hunter and also telling tall tales. One tall tale that he told was about being able to shoot a bullet at an axe and split it in half. Many of his tall tales describe things that were impossible. It seems silly that people believed the tales, but they did.

Davy Crockett married Mary Finley in 1806. His first son, John, was born in 1807. He had another son, William, in 1809. His only daughter, Margaret, was born in 1812.

Davy Crockett could not read or write until he was eighteen years old! He later became a soldier, and then a politician. He became a member of Congress in 1833. He died at the Alamo in 1836.

CORE SKILLS PRACTICE

The passage describes some of the events in Davy Crockett's life. Complete the timeline below by adding the event next to each year.

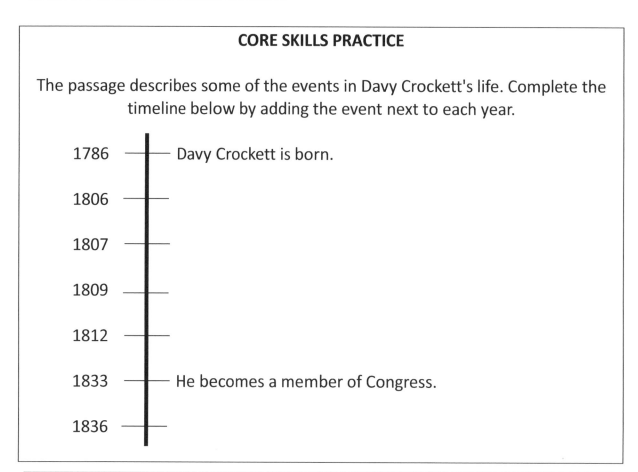

1786 — Davy Crockett is born.

1806 —

1807 —

1809 —

1812 —

1833 — He becomes a member of Congress.

1836 —

---

1 Read this sentence from the passage.

Many of his tall tales describe things that were impossible.

What does the word <u>impossible</u> mean?

- Ⓐ More possible
- Ⓑ Possible again
- Ⓒ Used to be possible
- Ⓓ Not possible

2 Which sentence from the passage is an opinion?

- Ⓐ *Davy Crockett was born on August 17th, 1786.*
- Ⓑ *He was born in Tennessee.*
- Ⓒ *It seems silly that people believed the tales, but they did.*
- Ⓓ *He later became a soldier, and then a politician.*

3 Which statement would the author of the passage most likely agree with?

- Ⓐ The tall tales are not really true.
- Ⓑ The tall tales should be believed.
- Ⓒ The tall tales have been proven correct.
- Ⓓ The tall tales should be tested again.

What is Your Color?

Today in class, we had a survey of eye color and hair color. I have black hair and green eyes. Fifteen people had brown hair, five had blond hair, three had black hair, and one person had red hair.

I am the only one in my class with green eyes. There were 15 people with brown eyes. That was more than half of the class. Only eight people had blue eyes. I think it's great that we live in a world with so many different kinds of people.

CORE SKILLS PRACTICE

Sometimes you will be asked to locate information in a passage. You can use this information to create a summary. Create a summary of the information in the passage by completing the tables below.

Hair Color	Number of Students
Brown	
Blond	
Black	
Red	

Eye Color	Number of Students
Green	
Brown	
Blue	

1   Read this sentence from the passage.

> **I think it's great that we live in a world with so many different kinds of people.**

Which word means the opposite of <u>different</u>?

    Ⓐ   Unusual

    Ⓑ   Similar

    Ⓒ   Rare

    Ⓓ   Unique

2   Which hair color was the most common in the class?

    Ⓐ   Brown

    Ⓑ   Blond

    Ⓒ   Black

    Ⓓ   Red

3   How is the narrator different from all the other students in her class?

    Ⓐ   She has black hair.

    Ⓑ   She has green eyes.

    Ⓒ   She liked the survey.

    Ⓓ   She has blue eyes.

4 Compare how common each hair color and eye color was. Use information from the passage to support your answer.

DIRECTIONS Be sure to:
- Write your answer in your own words.
- Write clearly.
- Check your answer after writing it.

_____

_____

_____

_____

_____

_____

_____

_____

Reading Comprehension

STAAR Reading

Set 3

Instructions

Read each passage. Complete the exercise under each passage.

Then complete the questions on the next page. For each multiple-choice question, read the question carefully. Then select the best answer. Fill in the circle for the correct answer.

Wishing Well

I am a coin in a well,
Here I was thrown and here I fell.
A little boy made a wish,
Now all of my neighbors are fish!
The day is coming around the bend,
When another wish will throw me a friend.

CORE SKILLS PRACTICE

The speaker of this poem is a coin. A coin does not really have feelings, but the poet gives the coin feelings. Use the information in the poem to answer the questions below.

How do you think the coin feels about being the only coin in the well?

_____

_____

_____

How do you think the coin will feel when another coin joins it?

_____

_____

_____

1   Which word best describes the mood of the poem?

     Ⓐ   Gloomy

     Ⓑ   Scary

     Ⓒ   Tired

     Ⓓ   Cheerful

2   Read this line from the poem.

The day is coming around the bend,

What does this line mean?

     Ⓐ   The day is coming soon.

     Ⓑ   The day will not come.

     Ⓒ   The day will be great.

     Ⓓ   The day is a long way away.

3   What is the rhyme pattern of the poem?

     Ⓐ   All the lines rhyme with each other.

     Ⓑ   There are three pairs of rhyming lines.

     Ⓒ   The first and last lines rhyme.

     Ⓓ   None of the lines rhyme.

Ducks

Ducks are small aquatic birds that live beside water. They can be found by both fresh water and sea water. They are found all over the world.

A male duck is called a drake. Female ducks are usually just called ducks, but can be called hens. Baby ducks are known as ducklings.

Ducks eat a variety of food including worms, plants, and small insects. Ducks have no nerves in their feet. This allows them to hunt for their food without being affected by the cold of the water.

CORE SKILLS PRACTICE

This passage has three paragraphs. Each paragraph has a different topic. Describe the topic of each paragraph. The topic of the first paragraph has been completed for you.

Paragraph 1: Where ducks live

Paragraph 2: _____

Paragraph 3: _____

1   Complete the web below using information from the passage.

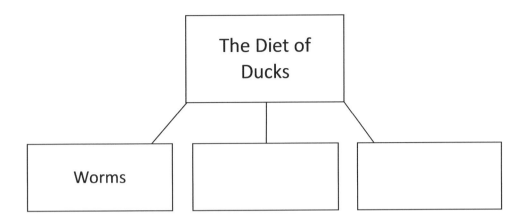

2   What is the second paragraph mostly about?

Ⓐ   Where ducks live

Ⓑ   What ducks eat

Ⓒ   What ducks look like

Ⓓ   Why ducks hunt

3   Based on the passage, where would a duck in a forest most likely be found?

Ⓐ   Near a river

Ⓑ   High in a tree

Ⓒ   On a grassland

Ⓓ   In the bushes

Careless Cooks

Aaron and Judy were making a cake. First they put in the flour and eggs. Next Judy found the cake tin while Aaron finished the cake mix. They poured it into the cake tin, put it in the oven, and went outside to play. They tired themselves out, so Aaron and Judy decided to go for a nap.

When they woke up, something smelled odd. They remembered their cake! It was too late. When they took it out of the oven, the cake was black and crunchy. Sadly, they had to throw it out.

CORE SKILLS PRACTICE

Sometimes you will be asked to give your opinion about something. This means that you will write about what you think. You can use information in the passage and your own knowledge to form an opinion. Give your opinion by answering the question below.

Aaron and Judy put the cake in the oven and then went for a nap. Do you think this was dangerous? Explain your answer.

_____

_____

_____

_____

_____

_____

---

1   Read this sentence from the passage.

They tired themselves out, so Aaron and Judy decided to go for a nap.

What does the word <u>nap</u> mean?

Ⓐ   Walk

Ⓑ   Play

Ⓒ   Sleep

Ⓓ   Drive

2   Where is most of the passage set?

Ⓐ   In a bedroom

Ⓑ   In a kitchen

Ⓒ   In a backyard

Ⓓ   In a dining room

3   Which of the following events happens last in the passage?

Ⓐ   Judy and Aaron have a nap.

Ⓑ   Judy and Aaron go outside to play.

Ⓒ   Judy and Aaron put the cake in the oven.

Ⓓ   Aaron finishes making the cake mix.

Day Dreaming

Sometimes I wonder what it would be like to be a bird. I would love to spread my wings and fly far and wide. I would fly all around the world. I would zoom across oceans to find new places.

First I would see the Pyramids in Egypt. Then I would drift over to England on a soft breeze to visit the Queen. I would perch on top of the Eiffel Tower in Paris. I would take in the view and pick my next place to visit. But for now, I just have to finish my homework.

CORE SKILLS PRACTICE

The author imagines what it would be like to be a bird. Think of an animal you would like to be. Write about what you would do if you were that animal.

_____

_____

_____

_____

_____

_____

_____

1   Read this sentence from the passage.

I would perch on top of the Eiffel Tower in Paris.

Which word means about the same as <u>perch</u>?

Ⓐ   Sit

Ⓑ   Rest

Ⓒ   Wait

Ⓓ   Dance

2   Which words does the author use to create a sense of great speed?

Ⓐ   *spread my wings*

Ⓑ   *zoom across*

Ⓒ   *drift over*

Ⓓ   *take in the view*

3   Complete the chart below using information from the passage.

Places to Visit	Thing to Do There
Egypt	
England	
Paris	Visit the Eiffel Tower

Glass

Glass is an everyday material found everywhere from bottles to windows. It is also recyclable. It is important to recycle glass because it means less new glass needs to be made. This saves a lot of chemicals from polluting the air. In fact, every metric ton of recycled glass saves 690 pounds of carbon dioxide polluting the air! Recycling glass also means that there is less waste.

Each state in America has its own system for recycling glass. Ask an adult in your state how you can help with recycling glass!

CORE SKILLS PRACTICE

The author gives reasons to support the idea that it is important to recycle glass. Describe two benefits of recycling glass.

1. _____

_____

2. _____

_____

1   Read this sentence from the passage.

In fact, every metric ton of recycled glass saves 690 pounds of carbon dioxide polluting the air!

Why does the author most likely include this sentence?

Ⓐ   To show how many uses of glass there are

Ⓑ   To describe a benefit of recycling glass

Ⓒ   To describe how glass is recycled

Ⓓ   To show that pollution is harmful

2   The author probably wrote this passage to –

Ⓐ   tell an interesting story about glass

Ⓑ   teach people about the uses of glass

Ⓒ   persuade people to recycle glass

Ⓓ   compare recycled glass with new glass

3   If the passage had another title, which title would best fit?

Ⓐ   Glass is Great

Ⓑ   How to Make Glass

Ⓒ   Start Recycling Glass!

Ⓓ   One Hundred Uses of Glass

4   Explain why it is important to recycle glass. Use information from the passage to support your answer.

DIRECTIONS Be sure to:

        - Write your answer in your own words.

        - Write clearly.

        - Check your answer after writing it.

_____

_____

_____

_____

_____

_____

_____

_____

Reading Comprehension

STAAR Reading

Set 4

Instructions

Read each passage. Complete the exercise under each passage.

Then complete the questions on the next page. For each multiple-choice question, read the question carefully. Then select the best answer. Fill in the circle for the correct answer.

Bananas

A banana is a type of fruit that grows on a tree. Bananas will grow in bunches on the tree. They are yellow and can be eaten as a snack or in meals or desserts. Wild bananas may contain seeds. However, the bananas grown on banana plantations* have been grown in such a way that they will not. When bananas are picked, they are green. While they are shipped all over the world, they ripen and turn yellow.

Notes
*Banana plantation – a banana farm

CORE SKILLS PRACTICE

Many passages include photographs. These support the information in the passage. Describe what the photograph helps the reader understand.

_____

_____

_____

_____

---

1   Based on the passage, what could be used to tell if a banana is ripe?

    Ⓐ   Its shape

    Ⓑ   Its size

    Ⓒ   Its color

    Ⓓ   Its seeds

2   What is the main purpose of the notes at the end of the passage?

    Ⓐ   To describe how bananas are grown

    Ⓑ   To show how to find more information

    Ⓒ   To give the meaning of a difficult term

    Ⓓ   To indicate the sources the author used

3   How are wild bananas different from bananas grown on banana plantations?

    Ⓐ   They may have seeds.

    Ⓑ   They are smaller.

    Ⓒ   They are green.

    Ⓓ   They grow faster.

The Desert Life

 The cowboy wandered through the desert. He and his horse Betty had been partners for four years. He liked the feeling of the sand in his boots. The smell of fresh cactus hung in the air. He didn't think he could have it any other way.

He lay down in the warm dirt with his hat resting on his chest. He watched the sun set to the west. The sky glowed orange, and then faded to pink.

"Life doesn't get much better than this," he said.

CORE SKILLS PRACTICE

The author helps the reader imagine what the desert is like by using different senses. The author describes what the cowboy sees, feels, and smells. List the details the author gives for each sense.

Sees: _____

_____

Feels: _____

_____

Smells: _____

_____

---

1 Read this sentence from the passage.

The cowboy wandered through the desert.

What does the word <u>wandered</u> suggest?

Ⓐ He walked a long way.

Ⓑ He was tired.

Ⓒ He was lost.

Ⓓ He walked slowly.

2 What is the mood of the passage?

Ⓐ Relaxing

Ⓑ Mysterious

Ⓒ Annoying ·

Ⓓ Confusing

3 Which word would the cowboy most likely use to describe his life?

Ⓐ Difficult

Ⓑ Pleasant

Ⓒ Easy

Ⓓ Exciting

One Dollar Bill

The most common form of currency in the United States is the one dollar bill. It was designed by Gilbert Stuart. It features a picture of George Washington on one side. The dollar bill was first issued in 1862. However, it looked much different than it does today. The dollar bill you see today wasn't introduced until 1969.

CORE SKILLS PRACTICE

A summary is a description of the main ideas in a passage. Write a summary of the passage by listing the main ideas.

_____

_____

_____

_____

_____

1   Read this sentence from the passage.

> **The most common form of currency in the United States is the one dollar bill.**

Which word means the opposite of <u>common</u>?

Ⓐ   Usual

Ⓑ   Popular

Ⓒ   Disliked

Ⓓ   Rare

2   Where would this passage most likely be found?

Ⓐ   In a book of poems

Ⓑ   In a magazine

Ⓒ   In a newspaper

Ⓓ   In a book of short stories

3   What is the main purpose of the passage?

Ⓐ   To instruct

Ⓑ   To entertain

Ⓒ   To persuade

Ⓓ   To inform

The Forest

The sun was setting in the sky. The moon was rising above the trees. For a few moments, the forest was still. Then came the crunching of dry leaves as all of the animals came out of hiding. The sound of twigs cracking filled the air.

The animals ran and danced in the cool night air. Fireflies circled above them, their lights twinkling like falling stars. The cold air was a relief after the humid day. The animals shouted and rejoiced at the beautiful night. The buzzing and chirping sounded like a beautiful song.

CORE SKILLS PRACTICE

The passage uses details that describe the sounds of the forest. Imagine you are sitting at a bus stop in a busy city street. Write a paragraph describing the sounds of the city.

_____

_____

_____

_____

_____

_____

_____

---

1   Read this sentence from the passage.

> **Fireflies circled above them, their lights twinkling like falling stars.**

Which literary device is used in this line?

Ⓐ   Personification

Ⓑ   Simile

Ⓒ   Flashback

Ⓓ   Metaphor

2   Which word from the passage describes what the forest sounds like?

Ⓐ   *crunching*

Ⓑ   *cool*

Ⓒ   *twinkling*

Ⓓ   *beautiful*

3   What is the setting of the passage?

Ⓐ   Early morning

Ⓑ   Early evening

Ⓒ   Late afternoon

Ⓓ   About midday

Neptune

 Neptune is one of the most interesting planets. It has been studied for many years. Yet scientists still do not know everything about it. Neptune was discovered in 1846 by Heinrich D'Arrest and Johann Galle. There are four gas planets in our Solar System. They are Jupiter, Saturn, Neptune, and Uranus. They are larger than all the other planets. Neptune is the smallest gas planet.

In August 1989, the Voyager spacecraft visited Neptune. It is the only time Neptune has been visited. It was discovered that, like Earth, the sky on Neptune has clouds in it. There are even some storms on Neptune.

CORE SKILLS PRACTICE

The author states that Neptune is an interesting planet. Do you think the author supports this statement well? How do you think the author could support this statement better?

_____

_____

_____

_____

_____

_____

---

1 Read this sentence from the passage.

> **Neptune was discovered in 1846 by Heinrich D'Arrest and Johann Galle.**

Which word could best be used in place of <u>discovered</u>?

Ⓐ Made

Ⓑ Found

Ⓒ Visited

Ⓓ Studied

2 How is Neptune different from Earth?

Ⓐ It has clouds.

Ⓑ It has storms.

Ⓒ It is a gas planet.

Ⓓ It is a smaller planet.

3 Which sentence from the passage is an opinion?

Ⓐ *Neptune is one of the most interesting planets.*

Ⓑ *Neptune was discovered in 1846 by Heinrich D'Arrest and Johann Galle.*

Ⓒ *Neptune is the smallest gas planet.*

Ⓓ *In August 1989, the Voyager spacecraft visited Neptune.*

4 What makes Neptune harder to study than other planets? Use information from the passage to support your answer.

DIRECTIONS Be sure to:
- Write your answer in your own words.
- Write clearly.
- Check your answer after writing it.

_____

_____

_____

_____

_____

_____

_____

_____

Reading Comprehension

STAAR Reading

Set 5

Instructions

Read each passage. Complete the exercise under each passage.

Then complete the questions on the next page. For each multiple-choice question, read the question carefully. Then select the best answer. Fill in the circle for the correct answer.

Finland

Finland is a country at the top of Europe. The total area of Finland is over 130,000 square miles. This makes Finland the eighth largest country in Europe. Its neighbors are Sweden, Norway, and Russia.

The capital of Finland is Helsinki. Helsinki is home to nearly 540,000 people. Finland's population as a whole is just over 5 million.

People in Finland most commonly speak Finnish or Swedish. Sometimes they will speak both.

CORE SKILLS PRACTICE

The passage includes many proper nouns. Proper nouns name a certain person, place, thing, or idea. Proper nouns always start with a capital letter. Complete the list of all the proper nouns in the passage.

Finland   Europe

_____   _____

_____   _____

_____   _____

1   Which of the following is NOT shown on the map?

  Ⓐ The size of Finland

  Ⓑ The capital of Finland

  Ⓒ The population of Finland

  Ⓓ The neighbors of Finland

2   Which language is commonly spoken in Finland?

  Ⓐ French

  Ⓑ English

  Ⓒ Italian

  Ⓓ Swedish

3   Where would this passage most likely be found?

  Ⓐ In a science magazine

  Ⓑ In a book of short stories

  Ⓒ In an encyclopedia

  Ⓓ In a travel guide

Fishy Dreams

One night as I lay in bed,
Dreams were spinning in my head.
I had a dream I was a fish,
I ended up in a dish!

I thought I would be someone's dinner,
I tried to make myself look thinner!
As I waited to walk the plank,
PLOP! I was placed in a fish tank!

CORE SKILLS PRACTICE

This poem is meant to be a funny poem. Describe two ways the poet creates humor in the poem.

1. _____

_____

2. _____

_____

1   What is the tone of the poem?

    Ⓐ   Sad

    Ⓑ   Angry

    Ⓒ   Playful

    Ⓓ   Gloomy

2   What is the rhyme pattern of each stanza of the poem?

    Ⓐ   Every line rhymes.

    Ⓑ   The second and fourth lines rhyme.

    Ⓒ   The first and last lines rhyme.

    Ⓓ   There are two sets of rhyming lines.

3   Read this line from the poem.

    I thought I would be someone's dinner,

What does this line mean?

    Ⓐ   I thought I would be eaten.

    Ⓑ   I thought I was hungry.

    Ⓒ   I thought I was a pet.

    Ⓓ   I thought I ate too much.

Harm's Diary

Dear Diary,

Today I went to the zoo again. I saw elephants, monkeys, penguins, and even a lion! But I think my favorite animal is now the alligator. It has dark scaly skin that makes it look a hundred years old. It looked a bit like a dinosaur too. But it was so big and fast. At first I was scared of it. It thrashed around when the zookeeper fed it. It had long white teeth like razors. It snapped its jaws together wildly. Mom told me that it could not climb the fence, so I was not afraid anymore. I knew I would be safe as long as I kept my hands away from the fence.

Until next time,

Harmanie

CORE SKILLS PRACTICE

What features described by Harmanie does the picture show?

_____

_____

_____

_____

---

1   Read this sentence from the passage.

It had long white teeth like razors.

The teeth are compared to razors to show that they were –

Ⓐ   shiny

Ⓑ   sharp

Ⓒ   metal

Ⓓ   thin

2   Why does Harmanie most likely keep her hands away from the fence?

Ⓐ   So she does not upset the alligator

Ⓑ   So she does not get bitten

Ⓒ   So she does not get her hands dirty

Ⓓ   So her hands do not get stuck in the fence

3   Which words does Harmanie use to suggest that the alligator was frightening?

Ⓐ   *dark scaly skin*

Ⓑ   *like a dinosaur*

Ⓒ   *snapped its jaws*

Ⓓ   *climb the fence*

Growing Pains

Spiders belong to the arachnid family. Arachnids are creatures that have no wings, eight legs, and have a body with two parts. Spiders do not have skeletons. Instead, they have a special skin that is known as an exoskeleton. The exoskeleton is hard enough to protect them.

As a spider grows, it needs a larger exoskeleton. Spiders shed their exoskeleton and stretch their bodies until a new exoskeleton forms. Once they stop growing, they do not need to shed their exoskeleton anymore.

CORE SKILLS PRACTICE

Use the information in the passage to answer the questions below.

What is an exoskeleton?

_____

_____

Why does a spider need an exoskeleton?

_____

_____

Why does a spider shed its exoskeleton?

_____

_____

---

1   Read this sentence from the passage.

The exoskeleton is hard enough to protect them.

Which meaning of the word <u>hard</u> is used in the sentence?

Ⓐ   Firm or tough

Ⓑ   Difficult

Ⓒ   Cruel or mean

Ⓓ   Powerful

2   Which sentence best describes what is shown in the picture?

Ⓐ   *Arachnids are creatures that have no wings, eight legs, and have a body with two parts.*

Ⓑ   *Instead, they have a special skin that is known as an exoskeleton.*

Ⓒ   *The exoskeleton is hard enough to protect them.*

Ⓓ   *As a spider grows, it needs a larger exoskeleton.*

3   What is the passage mainly about?

Ⓐ   A spider's legs

Ⓑ   A spider's exoskeleton

Ⓒ   A spider's bite

Ⓓ   A spider's web

Making Snowflakes

We're going to learn how to use borax to create a crystal snowflake.

Items

- Pipe cleaners
- String
- Heatproof jar
- Tablespoon
- Borax
- Pencil

Directions

1. Use pipe cleaners to create a snowflake shape.
2. Tie a piece of string to one of the edges of your snowflake.
3. Get an adult to pour boiling water into a heatproof jar.
4. Add three tablespoons of borax, one at a time. Mix the solution each time. Make sure the solution is clear before adding the next tablespoon.
5. Tie the string to a pencil. Then put it over the jar so the snowflake shape hangs inside, but does not touch the bottom.
6. Sit the jar overnight. Be sure to not move the jar for 24 hours.
7. Remove the snowflake from the solution and hang wherever you wish.

Remember to be careful when the water is hot!

1   Which of the following is completed first?

    Ⓐ   Sitting the jar overnight

    Ⓑ   Tying a piece of string to the snowflake

    Ⓒ   Adding borax to boiling water

    Ⓓ   Pouring boiling water into the jar

2   In which step is the jar first needed?

    Ⓐ   Step 2

    Ⓑ   Step 3

    Ⓒ   Step 4

    Ⓓ   Step 5

3   What is the purpose of the bullet points?

    Ⓐ   To describe the steps

    Ⓑ   To give safety warnings

    Ⓒ   To list the items needed

    Ⓓ   To show what a snowflake is

4   Why did the author write the passage? Use information from the passage to support your answer.

DIRECTIONS Be sure to:

- Write your answer in your own words.
- Write clearly.
- Check your answer after writing it.

_____

_____

_____

_____

_____

_____

_____

_____

_____

Reading Comprehension

STAAR Reading

Set 6

Instructions

Read each passage. Complete the exercise under each passage.

Then complete the questions on the next page. For each multiple-choice question, read the question carefully. Then select the best answer. Fill in the circle for the correct answer.

Independence Day

Tom's favorite holiday is Independence Day. However, most people call it the Fourth of July as that is the day it falls on.

Tom likes having a big dinner with his family. He also likes inviting his neighbors around. His neighbor Trisha always brings a delicious potato salad. Every year, Keith from across the street brings him a little American flag. Then his neighbor Mr. Bennett plays the piano for everyone.

CORE SKILLS PRACTICE

The passage describes how Tom's favorite holiday is Independence Day. What is your favorite holiday? Write a paragraph or two explaining what your favorite holiday is. Be sure to explain why it is your favorite holiday.

_____

_____

_____

_____

_____

_____

_____

---

1 Read this sentence from the passage.

His neighbor Trisha always brings a delicious potato salad.

Which word means about the same as <u>delicious</u>?

Ⓐ   Fresh

Ⓑ   Warm

Ⓒ   Pretty

Ⓓ   Tasty

2 Complete the chart below using information from the passage.

People that Visit Tom	What They Do
Trisha	Brings a potato salad
Keith	
Mr. Bennett	

3 Which word would Tom most likely use to describe Independence Day?

Ⓐ   Stressful

Ⓑ   Enjoyable

Ⓒ   Boring

Ⓓ   Unusual

The World's Oceans

An ocean is a large body of salt water. Approximately 70% of the Earth is covered by water. It is divided into a number of areas. The different areas of ocean include: Pacific Ocean, Atlantic Ocean, Indian Ocean, Southern Ocean, and the Arctic Ocean. The deepest point of the ocean is the Mariana Trench. The Mariana Trench is located in the Pacific Ocean.

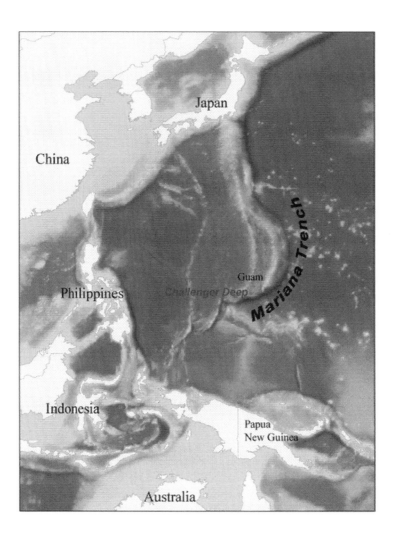

1   Read this sentence from the passage.

The deepest point of the ocean is the Mariana Trench.

Which word means the opposite of <u>deepest</u>?

Ⓐ   Fresh

Ⓑ   Strongest

Ⓒ   Shallowest

Ⓓ   Calmest

2   What is the main purpose of the passage?

Ⓐ   To instruct

Ⓑ   To entertain

Ⓒ   To persuade

Ⓓ   To inform

3   Which statement best describes what the map shows?

Ⓐ   How much of the Earth is covered by water

Ⓑ   What the five main oceans are

Ⓒ   How deep the Mariana Trench is

Ⓓ   Where the Mariana Trench is located

Fireworks

The fireworks flew high into the sky. Amazing colors lit up the sky in a sea of purple, green, blue, and orange. The crowd watched as a million rainbows shot out from nowhere.

The crowd was excited to see the amazing display, but Julie was scared. She had never seen a fireworks display and did not like the loud noises. She reached over to her mother and squeezed her hand. Her mother squeezed back and Julie felt a little safer.

CORE SKILLS PRACTICE

This story is written from a third person point of view. This means it is written by someone who is not part of the story. Now imagine that the story is written from Julie's point of view. Write a story about the fireworks from Julie's point of view. The first few sentences have been completed for you.

I felt scared as soon as the fireworks started. Everyone else was excited. I was

shaking. They were so loud. _____

_____

_____

_____

_____

_____

1   Read this sentence from the passage.

   The crowd watched as a million rainbows shot out from nowhere.

   Which literary device is used in this line?

   Ⓐ   Alliteration

   Ⓑ   Simile

   Ⓒ   Metaphor

   Ⓓ   Flashback

2   Which statement best describes what the passage is about?

   Ⓐ   A girl viewing her first fireworks display

   Ⓑ   A girl who is scared of everything

   Ⓒ   A girl spending time with her mother

   Ⓓ   A girl who wants to learn more about fireworks

3   What is the main purpose of the first paragraph?

   Ⓐ   To show how loud fireworks are

   Ⓑ   To describe what fireworks look like

   Ⓒ   To tell how Julie felt about the fireworks

   Ⓓ   To explain why Julie is at the fireworks display

Plastics

Every year 24% of plastics are recycled. This is a lower rate than newspapers. About 80% of newspapers are recycled. About 70% of fiberboard is recycled too.

One of the reasons that plastic is not recycled as often is that it is harder to recycle. There are many different types of plastic. They must be sorted before they can be recycled. Another issue is that many plastics have different colors used in them. This makes them harder to recycle.

It is still encouraged to place plastics in the recycle bin anyway. They will be sorted at recycling plants by workers. Then new items can be made with the old plastic.

CORE SKILLS PRACTICE

Many passages involve cause and effect. The cause is the reason for something. The effect is what happens because of the cause. Answer the question about the cause of something.

Why is plastic harder to recycle than paper?

_____

_____

_____

_____

_____

---

1   Read this sentence from the passage.

> **Another issue is that many plastics have different colors used in them.**

Which word could best be used in place of <u>issue</u>?

Ⓐ   Topic

Ⓑ   Solution

Ⓒ   Idea

Ⓓ   Problem

2   What is the main purpose of the second paragraph?

Ⓐ   To tell how plastic is recycled

Ⓑ   To explain why plastic is recycled less

Ⓒ   To show that plastic is not often recycled

Ⓓ   To encourage readers to recycle plastic

3   How are plastics different from newspapers?

Ⓐ   Plastics can be recycled.

Ⓑ   Plastics cannot be recycled.

Ⓒ   Fewer plastics are recycled.

Ⓓ   More plastics are recycled.

Australia

Australia is not only a country, but it is also a continent. In 1851, gold was discovered in Australia. This discovery led to many people traveling there from all over the world. By 1859, there were six colonies. In 1901, they agreed to form a commonwealth.

Australia now has 8 states and territories. They are Queensland, New South Wales, Northern Territory, South Australia, Victoria, Australian Capital Territory, Western Australia, and Tasmania. New South Wales has the largest population. It also has the largest city, which is Sydney. The capital of Australia is Canberra. It is in the Australian Capital Territory.

State or Territory	Number of People
New South Wales	7,200,000
Victoria	5,500,000
Queensland	4,500,000
Western Australia	2,300,000
South Australia	1,600,000
Tasmania	510,000
Australian Capital Territory	360,000
Northern Territory	230,000

CORE SKILLS PRACTICE

The table lists the states and territories in order. Explain how the states and territories are ordered in the table.

_____

_____

_____

1   Which state or territory is Canberra in?

   Ⓐ   New South Wales

   Ⓑ   Victoria

   Ⓒ   Australian Capital Territory

   Ⓓ   Northern Territory

2   Which detail from the article does the information in the table best support?

   Ⓐ   The largest city is in New South Wales.

   Ⓑ   Australia is a continent.

   Ⓒ   New South Wales has the largest population.

   Ⓓ   Australia had six colonies.

3   How is the passage mainly organized?

   Ⓐ   A solution to a problem is described.

   Ⓑ   A question is asked and then answered.

   Ⓒ   Facts are given to support an argument.

   Ⓓ   Events are described in the order they occurred.

4   Describe the major events in the history of Australia. Use information from the passage to support your answer.

DIRECTIONS Be sure to:
- Write your answer in your own words.
- Write clearly.
- Check your answer after writing it.

_____

_____

_____

_____

_____

_____

_____

_____

Reading Comprehension

STAAR Reading

Set 7

Instructions

Read each passage. Complete the exercise under each passage.

Then complete the questions on the next page. For each multiple-choice question, read the question carefully. Then select the best answer. Fill in the circle for the correct answer.

Vegetables

My dad has always said that I have to eat vegetables for my body to stay healthy. I never used to like vegetables much. I didn't really like the taste. So Dad decided to try something new to make sure I would eat them.

He started putting vegetables in dishes like spaghetti or inside pies. That way, I didn't even know I was eating vegetables. The funny thing was that I actually liked the taste. Now I no longer avoid vegetables. I am happy to eat them however they are served.

CORE SKILLS PRACTICE

Sometimes you will be asked to give your opinion about something. This means that you will write about what you think. Give your opinion by answering the question below.

Do you think the father's idea was a good one? Explain your answer.

_____

_____

_____

_____

_____

_____

1   Read this sentence from the passage.

Now I no longer avoid vegetables.

What does the word <u>avoid</u> mean?

Ⓐ   Dislike a lot

Ⓑ   Stay away from

Ⓒ   Agree to eat

Ⓓ   Identify or notice

2   How does the narrator learn to like vegetables?

Ⓐ   By learning that they are good for you

Ⓑ   By eating only small amounts

Ⓒ   By eating different types

Ⓓ   By eating them without knowing it

3   Which word best describes the narrator's father?

Ⓐ   Fussy

Ⓑ   Clever

Ⓒ   Mean

Ⓓ   Silly

Recycling

Recycling is really important. You can recycle glass, plastic, and paper. You put your trash made out of these materials into a special recycling bin. Then it is sorted by workers. After it is sorted, it is cleaned. Then it is made into new materials. In the end, your trash is turned into new items!

Recycling helps to save the environment. It helps because new glass, paper, and plastic doesn't need to be created. You should do your part and recycle! If everyone recycled, the world would be a better place.

CORE SKILLS PRACTICE

The first paragraph describes how trash is recycled. It describes the events in sequence, or in the order that the events happen. Think of a simple process that involves a few steps. It could be brushing your teeth or making your bed. Describe the steps in the process in order.

_____

_____

_____

_____

_____

_____

_____

1 What is the main purpose of the second paragraph?

Ⓐ   To explain how items are recycled

Ⓑ   To list items that can be recycled

Ⓒ   To encourage people to recycle

Ⓓ   To warn about the problems of recycling

2 What happens right after materials are placed into a recycling bin?

Ⓐ   The materials are thrown away.

Ⓑ   The materials are washed.

Ⓒ   The materials are sorted.

Ⓓ   The materials are turned into new items.

3 Which sentence from the passage is a fact?

Ⓐ   *Recycling is really important.*

Ⓑ   *You can recycle glass, plastic, and paper.*

Ⓒ   *You should do your part and recycle!*

Ⓓ   *If everyone recycled, the world would be a better place.*

View from the Moon

Many people believe that the Great Wall of China can be viewed from the Moon. This is actually incorrect. No manmade structures are visible from the Moon at all. Continents, oceans, and cloud cover can be seen. But structures like buildings and walls cannot be seen.

It is true that the Great Wall of China can be viewed from space. But so can many other structures. These include motorways, cities, landmarks, and even fields of crops.

CORE SKILLS PRACTICE

Why do you think the author wrote the passage? What is the main thing the author wants the reader to know?

_____

_____

_____

_____

_____

1   Read this sentence from the passage.

No manmade structures are visible from the Moon at all.

What does the word <u>visible</u> mean?

Ⓐ   Able to be seen

Ⓑ   Unable to be seen

Ⓒ   Able to be visited

Ⓓ   Unable to be visited

2   According to the passage, which of these can be seen from the Moon?

Ⓐ   Cities

Ⓑ   Motorways

Ⓒ   Crops

Ⓓ   Oceans

3   What is the most likely reason the Great Wall of China cannot be seen from the Moon?

Ⓐ   The Moon is too far away.

Ⓑ   The Moon is too dark.

Ⓒ   The Great Wall of China is too white.

Ⓓ   The Great Wall of China is in Asia.

Rookie

Today was my first day of basketball practice. We had to wear shirts that have numbers and our names on the back. One of the first things I learned is that bouncing the ball is called dribbling. When the coach first told us, I couldn't stop laughing about it! The coach told me to stop laughing. He said I should take basketball more seriously.

Most of the lesson was spent trying to throw the ball up and into the hoop. At first, the balls were going everywhere as if they had minds of their own. We learned that you can bounce the ball off the backboard. When it goes through the hoop, it's called getting a basket. I scored three baskets! I am excited for when I will be good enough to play my first game.

CORE SKILLS PRACTICE

In the passage, the author describes a day when he learned something new. Think of a time when you learned something new. Write a short description of that time.

_____

_____

_____

_____

_____

_____

1   Read this sentence from the passage.

He said I should take basketball more seriously.

What does the word <u>seriously</u> mean?

Ⓐ   In a way that is serious

Ⓑ   Not serious

Ⓒ   Less serious

Ⓓ   The most serious

2   What does the narrator find funny?

Ⓐ   That scoring is called getting a basket

Ⓑ   That the shirts have names and numbers on them

Ⓒ   That bouncing the ball is called dribbling

Ⓓ   That you can bounce the ball off the backboard

3   If the passage were given another title, which title would best fit?

Ⓐ   How to Be Good at Basketball

Ⓑ   Time to Get Serious

Ⓒ   Making the Team

Ⓓ   My First Try at a New Sport

Comets

Comets are balls of dust or ice that move through the atmosphere. They come from two different places in space. One is known as the Kuiper Belt. The other is known as the Oort Cloud.

Both of those locations are orbiting the Sun. But they are far from the Sun. The Kuiper Belt is just past Neptune. The Oort Cloud is about ten times farther from the Sun than Neptune.

They are so far away that the ice making up the comets does not melt. However, sometimes comets do come closer to the Sun. Then the ice begins to melt. This leaves a trail behind them. This gives comets their unique appearance.

CORE SKILLS PRACTICE

Locate the information in the passage to answer the questions below.

What is a comet made of?

_____

What planet is the Kuiper Belt just past?

_____

When does the ice of comets start to melt?

_____

---

1   Which of the following would be best to add to the passage to show the locations of the Kuiper Belt and the Oort Cloud?

Ⓐ   Table

Ⓑ   Graph

Ⓒ   Diagram

Ⓓ   Timeline

2   What does the illustration best show?

Ⓐ   Where comets are found

Ⓑ   The shape of comets

Ⓒ   What comets are made of

Ⓓ   How comets form

3   How is the Oort Cloud different from the Kuiper Belt?

Ⓐ   It is orbiting the Sun.

Ⓑ   It contains comets.

Ⓒ   It is nearer to the Sun.

Ⓓ   It is farther from Earth.

4   Explain why a comet looks like it has a trail behind it. Use information from the passage to support your answer.

DIRECTIONS Be sure to:

- Write your answer in your own words.
- Write clearly.
- Check your answer after writing it.

_____

_____

_____

_____

_____

_____

_____

_____

Reading Comprehension

STAAR Reading

Set 8

Instructions

Read each passage. Complete the exercise under each passage.

Then complete the questions on the next page. For each multiple-choice question, read the question carefully. Then select the best answer. Fill in the circle for the correct answer.

Take a Deep Breath

The lung is an organ that is used to help many living things breathe. Humans have two lungs in their body. The lungs have several important purposes. The main purpose of the lungs is to take in oxygen from the air. Carbon dioxide leaves the body via the lungs. The lungs are also used to protect the heart from any sudden shocks to the chest. Another purpose of the lungs is to filter blood clots.

Healthy Lungs

It is important to take good care of your lungs. One of the best ways to keep your lungs healthy is to exercise often. This gives your lungs a workout! The more you exercise, the stronger your lungs will become!

CORE SKILLS PRACTICE

Imagine that you are writing to a friend. You want to tell your friend how important it is to exercise. Write a paragraph explaining to your friend why it is important to exercise.

_____

_____

_____

_____

_____

1   Which sentence states the main idea of the first paragraph?

    Ⓐ   *Humans have two lungs in their body.*

    Ⓑ   *The lungs have several important purposes.*

    Ⓒ   *Carbon dioxide leaves the body via the lungs.*

    Ⓓ   *Another purpose of the lungs is to filter blood clots.*

2   What is the main purpose of the information in the box?

    Ⓐ   To give advice on how to have healthy lungs

    Ⓑ   To describe one of the purposes of the lungs

    Ⓒ   To describe the two human lungs

    Ⓓ   To show that lungs are important organs

3   Which of the following is NOT a purpose of the lungs?

    Ⓐ   Taking in oxygen

    Ⓑ   Protecting the heart

    Ⓒ   Filtering blood clots

    Ⓓ   Making energy

Friends in Far Places

My name is Dan. I have a pen pal who lives in France. His name is Jean-Luc. We talk about school, our pets, our families, playing sport, and many other things. Last week I sent him an American Flag and a penny in the mail. He sent back a chocolate bar and some stamps from his country. I took them to show and tell at school. All of my classmates were jealous. They asked if Jean-Luc had any friends to be their pen pals!

CORE SKILLS PRACTICE

If you could have a pen pal from any country, which country would you choose? Explain why you chose that country and what you would like to know about your pen pal's life.

_____

_____

_____

_____

_____

_____

_____

_____

1   Why were Dan's friends most likely jealous?

     Ⓐ   They wanted Dan to send them presents.

     Ⓑ   They wanted something from overseas for show and tell.

     Ⓒ   They wanted a pen pal from another country.

     Ⓓ   They wanted to visit France.

2   What did Jean-Luc send Dan?

     Ⓐ   A flag

     Ⓑ   A photograph

     Ⓒ   A chocolate bar

     Ⓓ   A penny

3   Complete the web below using information from the passage.

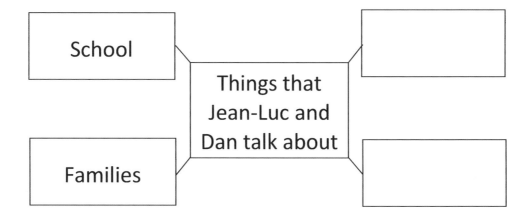

Making a Peg Doll

We are going to make a fun and cheap toy called a peg doll using wooden clothes pins. It is easy! Here is how you do it:

1. Use a marker to draw a face on the round end of the clothes pin.
2. Wrap a pipe cleaner around the center of the peg to give your doll arms.
3. Cut out a rectangle of paper or fabric to glue onto the doll for clothes.
4. Cut five pieces of wool and glue them to the head for the doll's hair.
5. Use the left over scraps of material, wool, or even add some glitter to make your doll look even better!

CORE SKILLS PRACTICE

Would you like to make a peg doll? Explain why or why not.

_____

_____

_____

_____

_____

1   Read this sentence from the passage.

> **We are going to make a fun and cheap toy called a peg doll using wooden clothes pins.**

Which word means the opposite of <u>cheap</u>?

Ⓐ   Easy

Ⓑ   Costly

Ⓒ   Serious

Ⓓ   Difficult

2   What is the pipe cleaner used to make?

Ⓐ   Face

Ⓑ   Hair

Ⓒ   Legs

Ⓓ   Arms

3   Which step is carried out first?

Ⓐ   Putting on hair

Ⓑ   Making clothes

Ⓒ   Drawing a face

Ⓓ   Adding arms

Pizza Night

Dear Grandpa,

Tonight we had pizza for dinner. My favorite food is pizza. Dad likes pepperoni pizza the most and Mom likes cheese pizza best. My favorite is ham and pineapple. What is your favorite type of pizza? Dad thinks people are strange for putting pineapple on a pizza. But I like the sweet taste. It is absolutely delicious! I hope I have pizza for dinner again soon. Well, I better get going.

Your granddaughter,

Sandy

CORE SKILLS PRACTICE

Sandy says that her favorite food is pizza. What is your favorite food? Write a paragraph describing what you like about that food.

_____

_____

_____

_____

_____

_____

1 Read this sentence from the passage.

> **Dad thinks people are strange for putting pineapple on a pizza.**

Which word means about the same as <u>strange</u>?

Ⓐ   Sweet

Ⓑ   Horrible

Ⓒ   Odd

Ⓓ   Mean

2 Use information from the passage to complete the table below.

Person	Favorite Type of Pizza
Sandy	Ham and pineapple
Dad	
Mom	

3 Who is telling the story?

Ⓐ   Grandpa

Ⓑ   Dad

Ⓒ   Mom

Ⓓ   Sandy

Better Than Expected

Rat was hiding in her little hole in the wall. She was curled up, playing with her whiskers. She heard the human family that lived in the house close the front door. This was her favorite time! She scurried around the human's kitchen finding tasty snacks. Then she saw Cat. She was so scared that she froze. Cat purred quietly and walked over to her. Rat began to cry.

"Don't cry Rat," Cat said. "Jump on my back and I can get you to the counter where the cheese is!"

CORE SKILLS PRACTICE

A summary is a description of the events of a story. A summary should include only the main events from the story. Write a summary of the story "Better Than Expected."

_____

_____

_____

_____

_____

_____

_____

1 Read this sentence from the passage.

She scurried around the human's kitchen finding tasty snacks.

What does the word <u>scurried</u> show about Rat?

Ⓐ She moved quietly.

Ⓑ She moved slowly.

Ⓒ She moved happily.

Ⓓ She moved quickly.

2 Which detail shows that the events in the passage could not really happen?

Ⓐ A cat talks to a rat.

Ⓑ A rat hides in a wall.

Ⓒ A human family leave the house.

Ⓓ A cat purrs quietly.

3 What would be most likely to happen next in the passage?

Ⓐ Rat would run back to her hole.

Ⓑ Rat would start crying again.

Ⓒ Cat would help Rat get to the cheese.

Ⓓ Cat would tell the human family about Rat.

4 What does the author want the reader to learn from Rat? Use information from the passage to support your answer.

> **DIRECTIONS** Be sure to:
> - Write your answer in your own words.
> - Write clearly.
> - Check your answer after writing it.

Answer Key

Core Skills Practice

The state standards for Texas are known as the Texas Essential Knowledge and Skills, or TEKS. These standards describe what students are expected to know. Student learning is based on these standards throughout the year, and the state test includes questions that assess whether students have the skills described in the standards.

Each passage in this workbook includes an exercise focused on one key skill described in the TEKS standards. The answer key identifies the core skill covered by each exercise, and describes what to look for in the student's response.

Reading Skills

The STAAR Reading test given by the state of Texas tests a specific set of skills. The answer key identifies what skill each question is testing. Use the skill listed with each question to identify areas of weakness. Then target revision and instruction accordingly.

The answer key also includes notes on key reading skills that students will need to understand to master the STAAR Reading test. Use the notes to review the questions with students so they gain a full understanding of these key reading skills.

Tracking Student Progress

Use the answer key to score the questions for each passage. After scoring the questions for each passage, record the score in the Score Tracker at the back of the book. Tally the scores to find the total once each set of 5 passages is complete.

As the student progresses through the sets, test scores will continue to improve as the students develops reading skills and gains confidence.

Set 1

A Close Match

Core Skills Practice
Core skill: Describe a character in a story
Answer: The student should explain that Adam is a good sport. The details that show this include that he shook Juan's hand, that he said "good game," and that he did not storm off the court.

Question	Answer	Reading Skill
1	C	Identify the meaning of phrases
2	A	Identify the main character
3	B	Identify and summarize the theme of a passage

Polar Bears

Core Skills Practice
Core skill: Write an informative text
Answer: The student should list questions that would be appropriate to answer in a report.

Question	Answer	Reading Skill
1	C	Identify the purpose of specific information
2	A	Identify the main idea
3	C	Draw conclusions based on information in a passage

Busy Bees

Core Skills Practice
Core skill: Identify nouns and proper nouns
Answer: Nouns: bees, world, honey bees, scientists, beekeepers, flowers, honey, beeswax
Proper nouns: Asia, Europe

Question	Answer	Reading Skill
1	Making honey Making beeswax	Summarize information given in a passage
2	A	Understand information in graphs, charts, or tables
3	B	Identify the author's main purpose

Scrambled Eggs

Core Skills Practice

Core skill: Analyze an author's technique

Answer: The student may describe how the writer uses an exclamation point, how the writer says positive things, or how the tone is encouraging.

Question	Answer	Reading Skill
1	C	Use context to determine the meaning of words
2	B	Use prior knowledge to draw conclusions
3	B	Identify the sequence of events

Crash Landing

Core Skills Practice

Core skill: Write a narrative

Answer: The student should write a description of an event from his or her day.

Question	Answer	Reading Skill
1	B	Use context to determine the meaning of words
2	C	Understand cause and effect
3	C	Identify different types of texts
4	See Below	Draw conclusions based on information in a passage

A complete answer should meet the criteria listed below. Give a score of 0, 1, 2, 3, or 4 based on how well the answer meets the criteria listed.

- It should give a well-supported explanation of why Stacey says that she is glad that her father makes her wear a helmet and knee guards.
- It should use relevant details from the passage.
- It should be well-organized, clear, and easy to understand.

Set 2

Paper Planes

Core Skills Practice

Core skill: Understand cause and effect

Answer: The student should explain that Terry gives up when his plane does not fly. The student should explain that the plane flies well when Ben adjusts it, or that Terry decides to keep trying when the plane flies well.

Question	Answer	Reading Skill
1	C	Understand and analyze literary techniques (simile)*
2	B	Make inferences about characters
3	A	Understand shades of meaning*

*Key Reading Skill: Simile

A simile compares two things using the words "like" or "as." The phrase "fell to the ground like it was made of lead" is an example of a simile.

*Key Reading Skill: Shades of Meaning

This question is testing vocabulary, but goes beyond basic word meanings to understand shades of meaning. Words have specific meanings, but words also have suggestive meanings. For example, the words *slender* and *skinny* both mean "thin." But the word *slender* suggests thin and attractive, while the word *skinny* suggests too thin. The word *glided* means "flew." But it also suggests that the plane flew smoothly.

My School Friends

Core Skills Practice
Core skill: Write an opinion piece
Answer: The student should give an opinion on whether or not it is important to have friends, and support the opinion with valid reasons.

Question	Answer	Reading Skill
1	B	Locate facts and details in a passage
2	B	Understand cause and effect
3	C	Compare and contrast characters

Dolphins

Core Skills Practice
Core skill: Identify factual details in a passage
Answer: The student should list four facts about dolphins. The facts include that they have fins, that they do not have gills, that they are related to whales and porpoises, that there are over 40 different species, that they live all over the world, and that they are carnivores.

Question	Answer	Reading Skill
1	B	Identify the author's main purpose
2	B	Compare and contrast two items
3	A	Identify details that support a conclusion

Davy Crockett

Core Skills Practice

Core skill: Summarize information in a passage

Answer: The student should complete the timeline with the details below.

          1806 - He marries Mary Finley.

          1807 - His son John is born.

          1809 - His son William is born.

          1812 - His daughter Margaret is born.

          1836 - He dies at the Alamo.

Question	Answer	Reading Skill
1	D	Use prefixes and suffixes to determine the meaning of a word*
2	C	Distinguish between fact and opinion*
3	A	Make inferences about an author's opinion or viewpoint

*Key Reading Skill: Prefixes and Suffixes

A prefix is a word part that is placed at the start of a word, such as *un-* or *dis-*. A suffix is a word part that is placed at the end of a word, such as *–less* or *-ly.* The word *impossible* is the base word *possible* with the prefix *-im* added to the start of the word. The meaning of *impossible* is "not possible."

*Key Reading Skill: Fact and Opinion

A fact is a statement that can be proven to be correct. An opinion is a statement that cannot be proven to be correct. An opinion is what somebody thinks about something. The sentence given in answer choice C is an opinion. It describes what the author thinks and cannot be proven to be true.

What is Your Color?

Core Skills Practice

Core skill: Summarize information in a passage
Answer: The student should complete the tables with the details below.
Hair color: brown 15, blond 5, black 3, red 1
Eye color: green 1, brown 15, blue 8

Question	Answer	Reading Skill
1	B	Identify and use antonyms*
2	A	Draw conclusions based on information in a passage
3	B	Compare and contrast two or more people
4	See Below	Summarize and evaluate information given in a passage

A complete answer should meet the criteria listed below. Give a score of 0, 1, 2, 3, or 4 based on how well the answer meets the criteria listed.

- It should correctly compare how common each hair color was.
- It should correctly compare how common each eye color was.
- It should use relevant details from the passage.
- It should be well-organized, clear, and easy to understand.

*Key Reading Skill: Antonyms

Antonyms are words that have opposite meanings. In this case, you are looking for the word that means "not different."

Set 3

Wishing Well

Core Skills Practice

Core skill: Make inferences about a character

Answer: The student should make a valid inference about how the coin feels and how the coin will feel when another coin joins it.

Question	Answer	Reading Skill
1	D	Identify the mood of a passage*
2	A	Identify the meaning of phrases
3	B	Identify the characteristics of poems

*Key Reading Skill: Mood

The mood of a passage is the way the passage makes the reader feel. It is the atmosphere of the passage.

Ducks

Core Skills Practice

Core skill: Identify main ideas

Answer: The student should identify the main topic of the second paragraph as being about what ducks are called, and the main topic of the third paragraph as being about what ducks eat.

Question	Answer	Reading Skill
1	Plants Insects	Summarize information given in a passage
2	B	Identify the main idea
3	A	Make predictions based on information in a passage

Careless Cooks

Core Skills Practice

Core skill: Form a personal opinion

Answer: The student should give an opinion about whether it was dangerous to put the cake in the oven and have a nap, and support the opinion with a valid explanation.

Question	Answer	Reading Skill
1	C	Use context to determine the meaning of words
2	B	Identify the setting of a passage
3	A	Identify the sequence of events

Day Dreaming

Core Skills Practice

Core skill: Write a narrative

Answer: The student should write a narrative about being an animal. Students should describe what they would do if they were that animal.

Question	Answer	Reading Skill
1	A	Identify and use synonyms
2	B	Understand and analyze word use
3	See the Pyramids Visit the Queen	Summarize information given in a passage

Glass

Core Skills Practice

Core skill: Identify supporting details in a passage

Answer: The student should list two of the benefits below.

- Less chemicals will pollute the air.
- Less carbon dioxide will be added to the air.
- There will be less waste.

Question	Answer	Reading Skill
1	B	Identify the purpose of specific information
2	C	Identify the author's main purpose
3	C	Identify the main idea*
4	See Below	Summarize and evaluate information given in a passage

A complete answer should meet the criteria listed below. Give a score of 0, 1, 2, 3, or 4 based on how well the answer meets the criteria listed.

- It should provide a valid and well-supported explanation of why it is important to recycle glass.
- It should use relevant details from the passage.
- It should be well-organized, clear, and easy to understand.

*Key Reading Skill: Main Idea

One way that identifying the main idea is tested is by asking what would be another good title for the passage. The correct answer is a title that describes what the passage is mainly about.

Set 4

Bananas

Core Skills Practice

Core skill: Interpret visual information

Answer: The student may explain that the photograph shows what a banana plant looks like, or that the photograph shows how bananas grow on plantations.

Question	Answer	Reading Skill
1	C	Draw conclusions based on information in a passage
2	C	Identify the purpose of text features
3	A	Compare and contrast two items

The Desert Life

Core Skills Practice

Core skill: Describe a setting

Answer: Sees: the sun setting, the color of the sky as the sun sets

Feels: sand in his boots, the warm dirt

Smells: fresh cactus

Question	Answer	Reading Skill
1	D	Understand shades of meaning*
2	A	Identify the mood of a passage*
3	B	Make inferences about characters

*Key Reading Skill: Shades of Meaning

Words have specific meanings, but words also have suggestive meanings. For example, the words *slender* and *skinny* both mean "thin." But the word *slender* suggests thin and attractive, while the word *skinny* suggests too thin. The word *wandered* means "walk." But it also suggests that the cowboy walked slowly.

*Key Reading Skill: Mood

The mood of a passage is the way the passage makes the reader feel. It is the atmosphere of the passage.

One Dollar Bill

Core Skills Practice

Core skill: Summarize a passage

Answer: The student should list the main ideas of the passage. The main ideas are listed
below.
- The one dollar bill is the most common form of currency.
- It was first issued in 1862.
- It was designed by Gilbert Stuart.
- It has George Washington on one side.
- The dollar bill seen today was first issued in 1969.

Question	Answer	Reading Skill
1	D	Identify and use antonyms*
2	B	Identify different types of texts
3	D	Identify the author's main purpose

*Key Reading Skill: Antonyms

Antonyms are words that have opposite meanings. In this case, you are looking for the word
that means "not common."

The Forest

Core Skills Practice

Core skill: Write a narrative

Answer: The student should write a narrative that describes the sounds of a city.

Question	Answer	Reading Skill
1	B	Understand and analyze literary techniques (simile)*
2	A	Understand and analyze word use
3	B	Identify the setting of a passage

*Key Reading Skill: Simile

A simile compares two things using the words "like" or "as." The phrase "lights twinkling like
falling stars" is a simile.

Neptune

Core Skills Practice

Core skill: Analyze main ideas and supporting details

Answer: The student should give an opinion on whether the author supports the idea that Neptune is an interesting planet. The student should describe how the statement could be supported better, such as by adding details that show that Neptune is special or interesting.

Question	Answer	Reading Skill
1	B	Use context to determine the meaning of words
2	C	Compare and contrast two items
3	A	Distinguish between fact and opinion*
4	See Below	Draw conclusions based on information in a passage

A complete answer should meet the criteria listed below. Give a score of 0, 1, 2, 3, or 4 based on how well the answer meets the criteria listed.

- It should provide a valid and well-supported explanation of why Neptune is harder to study than other planets.
- It should use relevant details from the passage.
- It should be well-organized, clear, and easy to understand.

*Key Reading Skill: Fact and Opinion

A fact is a statement that can be proven to be correct. An opinion is a statement that cannot be proven to be correct. An opinion is what somebody thinks about something. The sentence given in answer choice A is an opinion. It describes what the author thinks and cannot be proven to be true.

Set 5

Finland

Core Skills Practice

Core skill: Identify proper nouns

Answer: The student should list the proper nouns below.

Finland, Europe, Sweden, Norway, Russia, Helsinki, Finnish, Swedish

Question	Answer	Reading Skill
1	C	Understand and analyze information shown on maps
2	D	Locate facts and details in a passage
3	C	Identify different types of texts

Fishy Dreams

Core Skills Practice

Core skill: Analyze a poem

Answer: The student should describe two ways the poet creates humor. The student may refer to the fish wanting to look thinner, to the humor in the idea that a fish is worrying about being eaten, or to the use of exclamation points.

Question	Answer	Reading Skill
1	C	Identify the tone of a passage*
2	D	Identify the characteristics of poems
3	A	Identify the meaning of phrases

*Key Reading Skill: Tone

The tone of a passage refers to the author's attitude. It is how the author feels about the content of the passage. For example, the tone could be serious, sad, cheerful, or witty. In this case, the tone is playful.

Harm's Diary

Core Skills Practice

Core skill: Interpret visual information

Answer: The student may describe how the photograph shows the alligator's scaly skin, large size, large jaws, or long white teeth.

Question	Answer	Reading Skill
1	B	Understand and analyze literary techniques (simile)*
2	B	Draw conclusions based on information in a passage
3	C	Understand and analyze word use

*Key Reading Skill: Simile

A simile compares two things using the words "like" or "as." The phrase "white teeth like razors" is an example of a simile. This question is asking why Harmanie used this simile. Harmanie used it to show that the teeth were sharp.

Growing Pains

Core Skills Practice

Core skill: Locate facts and details in a passage

Answer: The student should answer the questions based on the information in the passage.
- An exoskeleton is a special hard skin on the outside of a spider.
- A spider needs an exoskeleton to protect it.
- A spider sheds its exoskeleton so it can grow larger.

Question	Answer	Reading Skill
1	A	Use words with multiple meanings*
2	A	Understand and analyze illustrations and photographs
3	B	Identify the main idea

*Key Reading Skill: Multiple Meanings

Some words have more than one meaning. These words are known as homonyms. All the answer choices are possible meanings for the word *hard*. The correct answer is the one that states the meaning of the word *hard* as it is used in the sentence.

Making Snowflakes

Question	Answer	Reading Skill
1	B	Identify the sequence of events
2	B	Understand written directions
3	C	Identify the purpose of text features
4	See Below	Identify the author's main purpose

A complete answer should meet the criteria listed below. Give a score of 0, 1, 2, 3, or 4 based on how well the answer meets the criteria listed.

- It should identify that the purpose of the passage is to instruct, provide directions, or teach people how to do something.
- It should include an explanation or evidence of how the student determined the purpose of the passage.
- It should use relevant details from the passage.
- It should be well-organized, clear, and easy to understand.

Set 6

Independence Day

Core Skills Practice

Core skill: Write an opinion piece

Answer: The student should name his or her favorite holiday and explain why it is his or her favorite holiday.

Question	Answer	Reading Skill
1	D	Identify and use synonyms
2	Brings an American flag Plays the piano	Summarize information given in a passage
3	B	Make inferences about characters

The World's Oceans

Question	Answer	Reading Skill
1	C	Identify and use antonyms*
2	D	Identify the author's main purpose
3	D	Understand and analyze information shown on maps

*Key Reading Skill: Antonyms

Antonyms are words that have opposite meanings. In this case, you are looking for the word that means "the least deep" instead of "the most deep."

Fireworks

Core Skills Practice

Core skill: Understand point of view

Answer: The student should complete the narrative. The narrative should be written in first person point of view.

Question	Answer	Reading Skill
1	C	Understand and analyze literary techniques (metaphor)*
2	A	Understand and analyze the plot of a passage
3	B	Identify the author's main purpose

*Key Reading Skill: Metaphor

A metaphor compares two things, or represents one thing as being another. In this case, the fireworks are represented as "a million rainbows." The fireworks are not actually a million rainbows, but are represented as a million rainbows. A metaphor is different to a simile because the words "like" or "as" are not used in a metaphor.

Plastics

Core Skills Practice

Core skill: Understand cause and effect

Answer: The student should explain that plastic needs to be sorted and that plastics have different colors used in them.

Question	Answer	Reading Skill
1	D	Use context to determine the meaning of words
2	B	Identify the author's main purpose
3	C	Compare and contrast two items

Australia

Core Skills Practice
Core skill: Understand and describe structure
Answer: The student should explain that the states and territories are in order from those with the highest number of people to those with the lowest number of people.

Question	Answer	Reading Skill
1	C	Locate facts and details in a passage
2	C	Understand information in graphs, charts, or tables
3	D	Identify how a passage is organized
4	See Below	Summarize information given in a passage

A complete answer should meet the criteria listed below. Give a score of 0, 1, 2, 3, or 4 based on how well the answer meets the criteria listed.

- It should summarize the main events described in the passage.
- It should use relevant details from the passage.
- It should be well-organized, clear, and easy to understand.

Set 7

Vegetables

Core Skills Practice
Core skill: Form a personal opinion
Answer: The student should give an opinion on whether or not the father's idea was a good one, and support the opinion.

Question	Answer	Reading Skill
1	B	Use context to determine the meaning of words
2	D	Understand and analyze the plot of a passage
3	B	Draw conclusions about characters

Recycling

Core Skills Practice
Core skill: Write an informative text
Answer: The student should describe the steps in a simple process in order.

Question	Answer	Reading Skill
1	C	Identify the author's main purpose
2	C	Identify the sequence of events
3	B	Distinguish between fact and opinion*

*Key Reading Skill: Fact and Opinion

A fact is a statement that can be proven to be correct. An opinion is a statement that cannot be proven to be correct. An opinion is what somebody thinks about something. The sentence given in answer choice B is a fact. All of the other sentences given are opinions.

View from the Moon

Core Skills Practice

Core skill: Determine the purpose or message of a passage

Answer: The student should explain that the main purpose of the passage is to explain that the Great Wall of China cannot really be viewed from the Moon.

Question	Answer	Reading Skill
1	A	Use context to determine the meaning of words
2	D	Locate facts and details in a passage
3	A	Make inferences based on information in a passage

Rookie

Core Skills Practice

Core skill: Write a narrative

Answer: The student should describe a time when he or she learned something new.

Question	Answer	Reading Skill
1	A	Use prefixes and suffixes to determine the meaning of a word*
2	C	Locate facts and details in a passage
3	D	Identify the main idea*

*Key Reading Skill: Prefixes and Suffixes

A prefix is a word part that is placed at the start of a word, such as *un-* or *dis-*. A suffix is a word part that is placed at the end of a word, such as *–less* or *-ly.* The word *seriously* is the base word *serious* with the suffix *-ly* added to the end. The meaning of *seriously* is "in a way that is serious."

*Key Reading Skill: Main Idea

One way that identifying the main idea is tested is by asking what would be another good title for the passage. The correct answer is a title that describes what the passage is mainly about.

Comets

Core Skills Practice

Core skill: Locate facts and details in a passage

Answer: The student should answer the questions based on the information in the passage.
- A comet is made of dust and ice.
- The Kuiper Belt is just past Neptune.
- The ice of comets melts when they come near the Sun.

Question	Answer	Reading Skill
1	C	Identify the purpose of text features
2	B	Understand and analyze illustrations and photographs
3	D	Compare and contrast two items
4	See Below	Identify cause and effect

A complete answer should meet the criteria listed below. Give a score of 0, 1, 2, 3, or 4 based on how well the answer meets the criteria listed.

- It should clearly explain why a comet looks like it has a trail behind it.
- It should clearly explain how the trail forms.
- It should use relevant details from the passage.
- It should be well-organized, clear, and easy to understand.

Set 8

Take a Deep Breath

Core Skills Practice

Core skill: Write an explanatory text

Answer: The student should explain why it is important to exercise. The student may explain how important the lungs are, and how exercising keeps the lungs healthy.

Question	Answer	Reading Skill
1	B	Identify the main idea
2	A	Identify the author's main purpose
3	D	Locate facts and details in a passage

Friends in Far Places

Core Skills Practice

Core skill: Write an opinion piece

Answer: The student should identify which country he or she would like a pen pal from. Students should include an explanation of why they would like a pen pal from that country.

Question	Answer	Reading Skill
1	C	Make inferences about characters
2	C	Locate facts and details in a passage
3	Pets Sport	Summarize information given in a passage

Making a Peg Doll

Core Skills Practice

Core skill: Form an opinion based on a passage

Answer: The student should explain whether or not he or she would like to make a peg doll, and provide reasons to support the opinion.

Question	Answer	Reading Skill
1	B	Identify and use antonyms*
2	D	Understand written directions
3	C	Identify the sequence of events

*Key Reading Skill: Antonyms

Antonyms are words that have opposite meanings. In this case, you are looking for the word that means "not cheap."

Pizza Night

Core Skills Practice

Core skill: Write an explanatory text

Answer: The student should name his or her favorite food. Students should clearly explain what they like about that food.

Question	Answer	Reading Skill
1	C	Identify and use synonyms
2	Pepperoni Cheese	Summarize information given in a passage
3	D	Identify point of view*

*Key Reading Skill: Point of View

This question is asking about the point of view of the passage. The passage has a first person point of view, which means that the story is told by a narrator. The narrator is Sandy. The other answer choices are people mentioned in the passage, but they are not telling the story.

Better Than Expected

Core Skills Practice

Core skill: Summarize a passage

Answer: The student should write a short summary of the story. The summary should include that the rat comes out of hiding to look for food, that the rat is scared by the cat, and that the cat offers to help the rat find food.

Question	Answer	Reading Skill
1	D	Use context to determine the meaning of words
2	A	Understand and analyze how realistic a passage is
3	C	Make predictions about characters
4	See Below	Identify the theme of a passage

A complete answer should meet the criteria listed below. Give a score of 0, 1, 2, 3, or 4 based on how well the answer meets the criteria listed.

- It should identify the main message of the passage as being about helping others, working together, not judging others, or not assuming the worst about others.
- It should use relevant details from the passage.
- It should be well-organized, clear, and easy to understand.

Score Tracker

Set 1

A Close Match	/3
Polar Bears	/3
Busy Bees	/3
Scrambled Eggs	/3
Crash Landing	/7
Total	**/19**

Set 3

Wishing Well	/3
Ducks	/3
Careless Cooks	/3
Day Dreaming	/3
Glass	/7
Total	**/19**

Set 2

Paper Planes	/3
My School Friends	/3
Dolphins	/3
Davy Crockett	/3
What is Your Color?	/7
Total	**/19**

Set 4

Bananas	/3
The Desert Life	/3
One Dollar Bill	/3
The Forest	/3
Neptune	/7
Total	**/19**

Score Tracker

Set 5

Finland	/3
Fishy Dreams	/3
Harm's Diary	/3
Growing Pains	/3
Making Snowflakes	/7
Total	**/19**

Set 7

Vegetables	/3
Recycling	/3
View from the Moon	/3
Rookie	/3
Comets	/7
Total	**/19**

Set 6

Independence Day	/3
The World's Oceans	/3
Fireworks	/3
Plastics	/3
Australia	/7
Total	**/19**

Set 8

Take a Deep Breath	/3
Friends in Far Places	/3
Making a Peg Doll	/3
Pizza Night	/3
Better Than Expected	/7
Total	**/19**

Texas Test Prep Practice Test Book

Get a head start on the STAAR Reading test taken by all grade 3 students! Get the Texas Test Prep Practice Test Book. It contains 8 reading mini-tests, focused vocabulary quizzes, plus a full-length STAAR Reading practice test.

Made in the USA
Charleston, SC
16 May 2014